THERE'S A SITUATION WITH ALLITERATION

BY

JACQUELINE JOSEPH-HINES

Alliteration

The use of the same beginnig consonant sound in a line or verse.

Cathy cautiously caught coughing copycats counting candy.

TABLE OF CONTENTS

INTRODUCTION

Alliteration is one of the most delightful and effective tools for helping beginning readers develop strong language skills. When words start with the same sound-like "giggling goats" or "dancing dolphins", children naturally tune in to the rhythm and music of language. This listening practice builds phonological and phonemic awareness, essential skills that help young readers recognize letter sounds and decode new words with confidence.

The playful patterns found in alliterative stories, rhymes, and tongue twisters capture children's attention while teaching them to hear the individual sounds that make up words. As they listen to and repeat these sound patterns, children strengthen the neural pathways that support reading success.

This book presents a journey through the alphabet, with engaging alliterative examples for each letter from A to Z. Each page offers opportunities for children to practice listening, speaking, and playing with language in ways that make learning both fun and meaningful.

April ate almonds, apples, and avocados as the astronaut announced Alexander alligator and Adam ant.

What Letter am I?

Alexander
the alligator

Adam
the ant

April

Bobby bit the banana, biking with Betzi and Betty as balloons and butterflies breezed by.

What letter am I?

Caleb, Colby, and Candi counted colorful caterpillars, cats, and cows while riding camels.

What letter am I?

Daniel and Dina docked on a desk full of donuts,
diamonds, dollars, and dimes.

What letter am I?

Ethel, Edith, Esther, and Eboni eat eggplant and eclairs every evening as elk, eagle, and elephant engage.

What letter am I?

Francis fixed fans and fences while Faith feasted on fish and fruit in the Fall.

What letter am I?

Godfrey gave gigantic gorillas, goats, and gophers gifts in the garden.

What letter am I?

Harlem happily handed horses hamburgers as Hanna and Henry hammered on the house.

What letter am I?

Inger, India, Ishmel, and Irma invited Ivan, Imani, and Iris to eat ice cream on Ivy Island as the iguana inched in.

What Letter am I?

Joseph and Jimmy joined jokingly in judo by the jeep as Jackson jumped joyfully with jellyfish and jets all around.

What letter am I?

Kelsey, Kylie, and Kendra kept kittens, kangaroos, and koalas flying kites by the kennel.

What letter am I?

Logan, Liam, and Layla laughed loudly, licking lollipops, holding lemons, and limes as lizards lay by the lake.

What letter am I?

Madison, Mason, and Miles moved mail, magazines, and mangos to the mat for mom.

What letter am I?

Nurse Nakita noticed numerous ninjas nabbing nuts and nectarines, and a nightingale napping in a nest.

What letter am I?

Ollie, Oscar, and Ophelia enjoyed oranges, olives, and oysters as Oppie Ostrich and Oliver Owl observed.

What Letter am I?

Palmer proudly placed pickles, pie, pizza, and peanuts in the painted plate as puppy, panda, panther, and pig pined patiently.

What Letter am I?

Queen Quilla, Quentin, and Quincy quieted the quadruplets sitting on the quilt giving a quarter.

What letter am I?

Rita and Reagan rocked and rowed their rowboat to reach raspberries and roses.

What letter am I?

Sallie and Sammy sorted seashells in the sand on the shore sensing sailboats sailing the sunny sea.

What Letter am I?

Tamika, Timmy, and Tasha took a turtle, two tigers, and teddy to telephone the teacher on Tuesday.

What Letter am I?

Usher, Urban, and Ursula rode unicycles with umbrellas underground wearing uniforms.

What Letter am I?

Venita viewed very vibrant violets as vultures ventured to the vines in the valley.

What Letter am I?

Witty Willow waded wildly in the water with wiggly worms and wobbly wallabies.

What Letter am I?

Xander, Xavier, and Xane saw a fox and an ox waxing a xylophone on a box.

What letter am I?

Yolanda yanked yellow yo yo's yelling at young
yaks before yielding a yacht.

What letter am I?

Zoey, Zelda, and Zuri zoomed a zeppelin, zucchinis, and zebras at the zoo.

What letter am I?

Alliteration All Around

Apple

Carrot

Ant

Airplance

Baby

Bear

Cow

Cat

Clock

Balloon

www.ingramcontent.com/pod-product-compliance
Lightning Source LLC
Chambersburg PA
CBHW052345210326
41597CB00037B/6263